ALWAYS REJOICING

A Verse by Verse Study of the Book of Philippians

John Goetsch

First published in 2008 by Striving Together Publications, a
ministry of Lancaster Baptist Church, Lancaster, CA 93535.
Striving Together Publications is committed to providing tried,
trusted, and proven books that will further equip local churches
to carry out the Great Commission. Your comments and
suggestions are valued.

Striving Together Publications
4020 E. Lancaster Blvd.
Lancaster, CA 93535
800.201.7748

Cover design by Andrew Jones
Layout by Craig Parker
Edited by Cary Schmidt
Special thanks to our proofreaders.

ISBN 978-1-59894-065-7

Printed in the United States of America

Table of Contents

An Instructional Greeting

Text

PHILIPPIANS 1:1–5

1   *Paul and Timotheus, the servants of Jesus Christ, to all the saints in Christ Jesus which are at Philippi, with the bishops and deacons:*
2   *Grace be unto you, and peace, from God our Father, and from the Lord Jesus Christ.*
3   *I thank my God upon every remembrance of you,*
4   *Always in every prayer of mine for you all making request with joy,*
5   *For your fellowship in the gospel from the first day until now;*

Overview

God desires that our lives as His people be filled with joy. The world with all of its temporal pleasures has no corner on happiness. *"Happy art thou, O Israel: who is like unto thee, O people saved by the* LORD, *the shield of thy help, and who is the sword of thy excellency! and thine enemies shall be found liars unto thee; and thou shalt tread upon their high places"* (Deuteronomy 33:29).

But while God has designed us to rejoice, that joy is a byproduct of our relationship with God. The word *blessed* is found seventy times in the book of Psalms and all but one of those times it literally means "happy." But notice the relationship that is emphasized in the opening verses of that great book: *"Blessed is the man that walketh not in the counsel of the ungodly, nor standeth in the way of sinners, nor*

5

sitteth in the seat of the scornful. But his delight is in the law of the LORD; *and in his law doth he meditate day and night"* (Psalm 1:1–2). Joy is never good without God!

Lesson Theme

The church at Philippi appears to have had very few problems and Paul gratefully rejoiced over what God had done in the lives of these believers. God's blessings, however, often bring Satan's attack. In these opening verses, Paul reminds the believers of their responsibility to continue living in obedience to God. The Christian life is never static. If we are not moving forward, we are sliding backward.

Introduction

_____

_____

_____

I. A Reminder of _____ (v. 1)

A. The _____ of God (v. 1A)

GALATIANS 6:10

10 As we have therefore opportunity, let us do good unto all men, especially unto them who are of the household of faith.

ECCLESIASTES 9:10

10 Whatsoever thy hand findeth to do, do it with thy might; for there is no work, nor device, nor knowledge, nor wisdom, in the grave, whither thou goest.

B. The _____ of God (v. 1B)

MATTHEW 23:12

12 And whosoever shall exalt himself shall be abased; and he that shall humble himself shall be exalted.

C. The _____ of God (v. 1C)

ACTS 20:28

28 Take heed therefore unto yourselves, and to all the flock, over the which the Holy Ghost hath made you overseers, to feed the church of God, which he hath purchased with his own blood.

1 THESSALONIANS 5:12–13
12 And we beseech you, brethren, to know them which labour among you, and are over you in the Lord, and admonish you;
13 And to esteem them very highly in love *for their work's sake*...."

II. The Results of _____ _____ (v. 2)

PROVERBS 28:14
14 Happy is the man that feareth alway: but he that hardeneth his heart shall fall into mischief.

A. Two _____ (v. 2A)

LAMENTATIONS 3:22–23
22 It is of the LORD's mercies that we are not consumed, because his compassions fail not.
23 They are new every morning: great is thy faithfulness.

JOHN 16:33
33 These things I have spoken unto you, that in me ye might have peace. In the world ye shall have tribulation: but be of good cheer; I have overcome the world.

PSALM 29:11
11 The LORD will give strength unto his people; the LORD will bless his people with peace.

ISAIAH 26:3
3   Thou wilt keep him in perfect peace, whose mind is stayed on thee: because he trusteth in thee.

B. Two _____ of the _____ (v. 2B)

JOHN 17:9–11, 23
9   I pray for them: I pray not for the world, but for them which thou hast given me; for they are thine.
10   And all mine are thine, and thine are mine; and I am glorified in them.
11   And now I am no more in the world, but these are in the world, and I come to thee. Holy Father, keep through thine own name those whom thou hast given me, that they may be one, as we are.
23   I in them, and thou in me, that they may be made perfect in one; and that the world may know that thou hast sent me, and hast loved them, as thou hast loved me.

JOHN 3:16
16   For God so loved the world, that he gave his only begotten Son, that whosoever believeth in him should not perish, but have everlasting life.

III. The Rejoicing in a _____ _____ (vv. 3–5)

A. A joyful _____ (v. 3)

PROVERBS 10:7
7   The memory of the just is blessed: but the name of the wicked shall rot.

PROVERBS 22:1
1   A good name is rather to be chosen than great riches, and loving favour rather than silver and gold.

B. A joyful _____ *(v. 4)*

HEBREWS 7:25
25   Wherefore he is able also to save them to the uttermost that come unto God by him, seeing he ever liveth to make intercession for them.

C. A joyful _____ *(v. 5)*

GALATIANS 3:28
28   There is neither Jew nor Greek, there is neither bond nor free, there is neither male nor female: for ye are all one in Christ Jesus.

MATTHEW 18:15–20
15   Moreover if thy brother shall trespass against thee, go and tell him his fault between thee and him alone: if he shall hear thee, thou hast gained thy brother.
16   But if he will not hear thee, then take with thee one or two more, that in the mouth of two or three witnesses every word may be established.
17   And if he shall neglect to hear them, tell it unto the church: but if he neglect to hear the church, let him be unto thee as an heathen man and a publican.
18   Verily I say unto you, Whatsoever ye shall bind on earth shall be bound in heaven: and whatsoever ye shall loose on earth shall be loosed in heaven.
19   Again I say unto you, That if two of you shall agree on earth as touching any thing that they shall ask, it shall be done for them of my Father which is in heaven.

20   For where two or three are gathered together in my name, there am I in the midst of them.

Conclusion

Study Questions

1. Who wrote the book of Philippians?

2. According to John 15:9–11, joy is coupled with which command?

3. What common theme is seen in the following Scriptures: Philippians 1:1, 2 Corinthians 4:5, and Galatians 6:10.

4. Using Psalm 16:11, explain the following statement: "True joy is a byproduct of our relationship with God."

5. Think of the name of Jesus Christ, and write down the first three words that come to your mind. When other people think of your name, what three words do you wish they would write down? Compare your answers.

6. Instead of criticizing or fighting with God and His people, we ought to be exercising ourselves *"to have always a conscience void of offence toward God, and toward men"* (Acts 24:16). If the following scenario were to happen to you, what should your response be? Your pastor asked you to organize a small luncheon for some first-time visitors. After gathering some church members to help, you delegate responsibilities and begin preparing for this fellowship time. A day before the luncheon, the church member in charge of decorating for the luncheon calls you and tells you that she has not done anything for the luncheon and is just too busy to help. How should you respond to this child of God?

7. According to Matthew 18:15–20, when we are not right with a fellow Christian, the work of God is bound on earth and is also bound in Heaven. What relationship do you need to mend or better so that your prayers may be answered? What steps can you take to biblically mend this relationship?

8. Consider your position in the local church. By taking inventory of your priorities, determine if you are an asset to your local church or a liability. Explain your answer.

Memory Verse

PHILIPPIANS 1:3–4

3   *I thank my God upon every remembrance of you,*
4   *Always in every prayer of mine for you all making request with joy,*

An Inspirational Goal

Text

PHILIPPIANS 1:6–26

6   Being confident of this very thing, that he which hath begun a good work in you will perform it until the day of Jesus Christ:

7   Even as it is meet for me to think this of you all, because I have you in my heart; inasmuch as both in my bonds, and in the defence and confirmation of the gospel, ye all are partakers of my grace.

8   For God is my record, how greatly I long after you all in the bowels of Jesus Christ.

9   And this I pray, that your love may abound yet more and more in knowledge and in all judgment;

10   That ye may approve things that are excellent; that ye may be sincere and without offence till the day of Christ;

11   Being filled with the fruits of righteousness, which are by Jesus Christ, unto the glory and praise of God.

12   But I would ye should understand, brethren, that the things which happened unto me have fallen out rather unto the furtherance of the gospel;

13   So that my bonds in Christ are manifest in all the palace, and in all other places;

14   And many of the brethren in the Lord, waxing confident by my bonds, are much more bold to speak the word without fear.

15   Some indeed preach Christ even of envy and strife; and some also of good will:

16   The one preach Christ of contention, not sincerely, supposing to add affliction to my bonds:

17 *But the other of love, knowing that I am set for the defence of the gospel.*

18 *What then? notwithstanding, every way, whether in pretence, or in truth, Christ is preached; and I therein do rejoice, yea, and will rejoice.*

19 *For I know that this shall turn to my salvation through your prayer, and the supply of the Spirit of Jesus Christ,*

20 *According to my earnest expectation and my hope, that in nothing I shall be ashamed, but that with all boldness, as always, so now also Christ shall be magnified in my body, whether it be by life, or by death.*

21 *For to me to live is Christ, and to die is gain.*

22 *But if I live in the flesh, this is the fruit of my labour: yet what I shall choose I wot not.*

23 *For I am in a strait betwixt two, having a desire to depart, and to be with Christ; which is far better:*

24 *Nevertheless to abide in the flesh is more needful for you.*

25 *And having this confidence, I know that I shall abide and continue with you all for your furtherance and joy of faith;*

26 *That your rejoicing may be more abundant in Jesus Christ for me by my coming to you again.*

Overview

While the church at Philippi was a strong and fruitful church, Paul did not want them to become apathetic and unproductive. The Christian life is described throughout Scripture as a growing relationship with Christ. In these next verses, the Apostle challenges these believers with some spiritual goals. Each time that Paul returned to these believers, he desired to find them in a closer relationship with Christ and accomplishing greater ministry for God's glory.

Lesson Theme

Setting goals in our lives spiritually is important if we want to accomplish something for God, but it is vital that these goals are what God wants and not our own agenda. The model prayer of Jesus is our supreme example of selflessness: *"...nevertheless not as I will, but as thou wilt"* (Matthew 26:39B). The choice is not simply to have goals, but rather, whose goals? *"Know ye not, that to whom ye yield yourselves servants to obey, his servants ye are to whom ye obey; whether of sin unto death, or of obedience unto righteousness?"* (Romans 6:16).

The goal of every child of God ought to become less and less like the world and more and more centered in God's will. *"And be not conformed to this world: but be ye transformed by the renewing of your mind, that ye may prove what is that good, and acceptable, and perfect, will of God"* (Romans 12:2). By the way, it's hard to improve on *perfect!*

Introduction

_____

_____

_____

1 CORINTHIANS 10:31
31 *Whether therefore ye eat, or drink, or whatsoever ye do, do all to the glory of God.*

I. An Approved _____ (vv. 6–11)

A. *We serve a* _____.*(v. 6)*

ROMANS 1:25
25 *Who changed the truth of God into a lie, and worshipped and served the creature more than the Creator, who is blessed for ever. Amen.*

JOHN 3:19–20
19 *And this is the condemnation, that light is come into the world, and men loved darkness rather than light, because their deeds were evil.*
20 *For every one that doeth evil hateth the light, neither cometh to the light, lest his deeds should be reproved.*

PSALM 102:25–27
25 *Of old hast thou laid the foundation of the earth: and the heavens are the work of thy hands.*
26 *They shall perish, but thou shalt endure: yea, all of them shall wax old like a garment; as a vesture shalt thou change them, and they shall be changed:*

27 But thou art the same, and thy years shall have no end.

B. We strive for _____. *(vv. 7–9)*

2 Peter 3:18a
18 But grow in grace, and in the knowledge of our Lord and Saviour Jesus Christ.

1 Peter 2:2
2 As newborn babes, desire the sincere milk of the word, that ye may grow thereby:

Ephesians 3:17–19
17 That Christ may dwell in your hearts by faith; that ye, being rooted and grounded in love,
18 May be able to comprehend with all saints what is the breadth, and length, and depth, and height;
19 And to know the love of Christ, which passeth knowledge, that ye might be filled with all the fulness of God.

C. We seek a _____. *(vv. 10–11)*

2 Corinthians 3:5
5 Not that we are sufficient of ourselves to think any thing as of ourselves; but our sufficiency is of God;

Ephesians 4:13–15
13 Till we all come in the unity of the faith, and of the knowledge of the Son of God, unto a perfect man, unto the measure of the stature of the fulness of Christ:
14 That we henceforth be no more children, tossed to and fro, and carried about with every wind of doctrine, by the sleight of men, and cunning craftiness, whereby they lie in wait to deceive;

15   But speaking the truth in love, may grow up into him in all things, which is the head, even Christ:

ACTS 11:26B
26   And the disciples were called Christians first in Antioch.

2 PETER 1:4
4   Whereby are given unto us exceeding great and precious promises: that by these ye might be partakers of the divine nature, having escaped the corruption that is in the world through lust.

II. An Appointed _____ (vv. 12–14)

ROMANS 8:28
28   And we know that all things work together for good to them that love God, to them who are the called according to his purpose.

A. Paul's _____ produced a bigger _____. (v. 12)

B. Paul's _____ produced a broader _____. (v. 13)

C. Paul's _____ produced a bolder _____. (v. 14)

2 CORINTHIANS 3:2–3
2   Ye are our epistle written in our hearts, known and read of all men:

3   Forasmuch as ye are manifestly declared to be the
epistle of Christ ministered by us, written not with ink,
but with the Spirit of the living God; not in tables of
stone, but in fleshy tables of the heart.

HEBREWS 12:2–3
2   Looking unto Jesus the author and finisher of our
faith; who for the joy that was set before him endured
the cross, despising the shame, and is set down at the
right hand of the throne of God.
3   For consider him that endured such contradiction
of sinners against himself, lest ye be wearied and faint
in your minds.

III. An Apparent _____ (vv. 15–18)

A. The _____ over an improper motive (vv. 15–17)

ISAIAH 29:13
13   Wherefore the Lord said, Forasmuch as this people
draw near me with their mouth, and with their lips
do honour me, but have removed their heart far from
me, and their fear toward me is taught by the precept
of men:

B. The _____ for an impeccable message (v. 18)

ISAIAH 55:10–11
10   For as the rain cometh down, and the snow from
heaven, and returneth not thither, but watereth the

earth, and maketh it bring forth and bud, that it may give seed to the sower, and bread to the eater:
11 So shall my word be that goeth forth out of my mouth: it shall not return unto me void, but it shall accomplish that which I please, and it shall prosper in the thing whereto I sent it.

ISAIAH 34:16A
16 Seek ye out of the book of the LORD, and read: no one of these shall fail,

IV. An Assured _____ (vv. 19–26)

ACTS 20:24
24 But none of these things move me, neither count I my life dear unto myself, so that I might finish my course with joy, and the ministry, which I have received of the Lord Jesus, to testify the gospel of the grace of God.

1 CORINTHIANS 15:58
58 Therefore, my beloved brethren, be ye stedfast, unmoveable, always abounding in the work of the Lord, forasmuch as ye know that your labour is not in vain in the Lord.

A. Two strengthening _____ (v. 19)

ROMANS 8:26
26 Likewise the Spirit also helpeth our infirmities: for we know not what we should pray for as we ought: but the Spirit itself maketh intercession for us with groanings which cannot be uttered.

LUKE 11:13

13 If ye then, being evil, know how to give good gifts unto your children: how much more shall your heavenly Father give the Holy Spirit to them that ask him?

B. Two sobering _____ *(v. 20)*

1 JOHN 2:28

28 And now, little children, abide in him; that, when he shall appear, we may have confidence, and not be ashamed before him at his coming.

JOHN 8:29–30

29 And he that sent me is with me: the Father hath not left me alone; for I do always those things that please him.

30 As he spake these words, many believed on him.

C. Two sovereign _____ *(vv. 21–26)*

Conclusion

_____

_____

_____

Study Questions

1. According to 1 Corinthians 10:31, what should be the goal of every Christian?

2. Do you have a genuine desire to grow spiritually? If so, write out and consider the challenge given by the prophet in Isaiah 54:2.

3. Why is becoming like Christ impossible without His help according to 2 Corinthians 3:5?

4. Isaac D'Israeli once wrote, "...it is a wretched taste to be gratified with mediocrity when the excellent lies before us." List three areas in your life that you would consider to be mediocre, and in what ways you can improve.

5. Are you willing to receive from God's hand anything that He chooses to give to you? If God chose to take your eyesight and give you a life of blindness, how would Romans 8:28 apply to this scenario?

6. Think of a personal trial that God put into your life. How can that trial be used for a greater impact?

7. If you could have two tools to help you live your Christian life, what would they be?

   Compare your answers with the Apostle Paul's request in Philippians 1:19. What two tools did he ask for?

8. Jonathan Edwards once said, "So live, so that should you suddenly die you would not be ashamed." If your life had suddenly ended in the past twenty-four hours, would you have been ashamed to die doing what you were doing? Or thinking what you were thinking? Or dreaming what you were dreaming? Explain your answer.

Memory Verse
PHILIPPIANS 1:6
6 Being confident of this very thing, that he which hath begun a good work in you will perform it until the day of Jesus Christ:

An Increasing Godliness

Text

PHILIPPIANS 1:27–30

27 Only let your conversation be as it becometh the gospel of Christ: that whether I come and see you, or else be absent, I may hear of your affairs, that ye stand fast in one spirit, with one mind striving together for the faith of the gospel;

28 And in nothing terrified by your adversaries: which is to them an evident token of perdition, but to you of salvation, and that of God.

29 For unto you it is given in the behalf of Christ, not only to believe on him, but also to suffer for his sake;

30 Having the same conflict which ye saw in me, and now hear to be in me.

Overview

It is our responsibility as Christians to become like Christ in every area of our lives. While this may sound lofty in its ideal, it is possible through the power that is working in us. Many religions and philosophies focus on changing the outside of man, but Christ in us enables us to change from the inside out. When Christ dwells *in* us and His presence is understood and obeyed, the *outside* will soon conform to His will as well.

Lesson Theme

An Increasing Godliness ought to be the desire of every child of God. Is it possible to be godly in such a wicked world? Can God really change a person who is dominated by his old sinful nature within? We are going to discover some practical ways in which we can walk in the spirit and thus not fulfill the lusts of our flesh.

Introduction

_____

_____

_____

I. Christ-like in _____ (v. 27)

1 SAMUEL 16:7B

7   *...for the LORD seeth not as man seeth; for man looketh on the outward appearance, but the LORD looketh on the heart.*

A. A comprehensive _____ (v. 27A)

B. A compelling _____ (v. 27B)

JOHN 1:19–23

19   And this is the record of John, when the Jews sent priests and Levites from Jerusalem to ask him, Who art thou?

20   And he confessed, and denied not; but confessed, I am not the Christ.

21   And they asked him, What then? Art thou Elias? And he saith, I am not. Art thou that prophet? And he answered, No.

22   Then said they unto him, Who art thou? that we may give an answer to them that sent us. What sayest thou of thyself?

23   He said, I am the voice of one crying in the wilderness, Make straight the way of the Lord, as said the prophet Esaias.

C. A consistent _____ (v. 27C)

II. Christ-like in _____ (v. 27)

ACTS 2:46–47

46 And they, continuing daily with one accord in the temple, and breaking bread from house to house, did eat their meat with gladness and singleness of heart,

47 Praising God, and having favour with all the people. And the Lord added to the church daily such as should be saved.

A. A oneness in _____ (v. 27D)

PROVERBS 20:27

27 The spirit of man is the candle of the LORD, searching all the inward parts of the belly.

ACTS 24:16

16 And herein do I exercise myself, to have always a conscience void of offence toward God, and toward men.

B. A oneness in _____ (v. 27E)

C. A oneness in _____ (v. 27F)

1 CORINTHIANS 3:3–9A

3 For ye are yet carnal: for whereas there is among you envying, and strife, and divisions, are ye not carnal, and walk as men?

4 For while one saith, I am of Paul; and another, I am of Apollos; are ye not carnal?

5 Who then is Paul, and who is Apollos, but ministers by whom ye believed, even as the Lord gave to every man?

6 I have planted, Apollos watered; but God gave the increase.

7   So then neither is he that planteth any thing, neither he that watereth; but God that giveth the increase.

8   Now he that planteth and he that watereth are one: and every man shall receive his own reward according to his own labour.

9   For we are labourers together with God:...

III. Christ-like in _____ (vv. 28–30)

1 PETER 5:8

8   Be sober, be vigilant; because your adversary the devil, as a roaring lion, walketh about, seeking whom he may devour:

A. The _____ of Satan (v. 28A)

HEBREWS 2:14

14   Forasmuch then as the children are partakers of flesh and blood, he also himself likewise took part of the same; that through death he might destroy him that had the power of death, that is, the devil;

REVELATION 20:10

10   And the devil that deceived them was cast into the lake of fire and brimstone, where the beast and the false prophet are, and shall be tormented day and night for ever and ever.

JAMES 4:7

7   Submit yourselves therefore to God. Resist the devil, and he will flee from you.

B. The _____ of salvation (v. 28B)

John 8:32–36

32   And ye shall know the truth, and the truth shall
make you free.

33   They answered him, We be Abraham's seed, and
were never in bondage to any man: how sayest thou,
Ye shall be made free?

34   Jesus answered them, Verily, verily, I say unto you,
Whosoever committeth sin is the servant of sin.

35   And the servant abideth not in the house for ever:
but the Son abideth ever.

36   If the Son therefore shall make you free, ye shall
be free indeed.

C. The _____ of suffering (vv. 29–30)

1 Peter 1:7

7   That the trial of your faith, being much more
precious than of gold that perisheth, though it be tried
with fire, might be found unto praise and honour and
glory at the appearing of Jesus Christ:

Conclusion

_____

_____

_____

Study Questions

1. Define the word *conversation* in Philippians 1:27.

2. Divisiveness always starts in the attitude rather than the actions. How can the truth in Acts 24:16 help you maintain a right spirit so you do not fall prey to contention?

3. What admonition does James give in James 5:16A?

4. Because strife comes into a family or a church when agendas clash, the Apostle Paul encourages us to be in one mind (Philippians 1:27). In contrast, how does Proverbs 12:15 describe one who does that which is right in his own eyes?

5. Write out and explain the command the Apostle Paul gives in Romans 12:16.

6. When you are faced with a fear or temptation beyond your strength to withstand, cling to Someone stronger and mightier than you. Take out a 3x5 card, and write the following verses and reminders down. Use this

card the next time a strong fear or temptation crosses your path.

> 1 John 4:4, "...*greater is he that is in you, than he that is in the world.*" Satan's ploys are no match for the Saviour's power. When Satan comes calling, let Christ answer the door. Whenever you come under the pressure of Satan, meditate on the presence of your Saviour. James 4:7, "*Submit yourselves therefore to God. Resist the devil, and he will flee from you.*"

7. Too many Christians live as though they have never been freed from the bondage of sin. Read Romans 6:6, and make a list of sins you feel have bondage over you.

8. Read Romans 6:7–18. Write three verses in this passage that will help you have victory over the sins that seem to bind you. Reread verse eighteen, and be reminded that Christ has freed you from the bondage of sin and has called you to righteousness.

Memory Verse

PHILIPPIANS 1:27

27 *Only let your conversation be as it becometh the gospel of Christ: that whether I come and see you, or else be absent, I may hear of your affairs, that ye stand fast in one spirit, with one mind striving together for the faith of the gospel;*

A New Nature Expressed

Text

PHILIPPIANS 2:1–8

1   If there be therefore any consolation in Christ, if any comfort of love, if any fellowship of the Spirit, if any bowels and mercies,

2   Fulfil ye my joy, that ye be likeminded, having the same love, being of one accord, of one mind.

3   Let nothing be done through strife or vainglory; but in lowliness of mind let each esteem other better than themselves.

4   Look not every man on his own things, but every man also on the things of others.

5   Let this mind be in you, which was also in Christ Jesus:

6   Who, being in the form of God, thought it not robbery to be equal with God:

7   But made himself of no reputation, and took upon him the form of a servant, and was made in the likeness of men:

8   And being found in fashion as a man, he humbled himself, and became obedient unto death, even the death of the cross.

Overview

This is one of the most important sections in the book of Philippians and perhaps in all of Scripture. While there is a good deal of doctrinal content in this passage, we will focus our attention on the practical side in this lesson. Jesus *"came not to be ministered unto, but to minister, and to give his life a ransom for many"* (Matthew 20:28B). The fruit of our new nature in Christ ought to be expressed in service to God and to others.

Lesson Theme

The "seeker-sensitive" church movement seeks to entertain it's members with all kinds of programs, technology, and feel-good theology. God, however, has saved us to serve and it is the job of the local church to equip and engage people in the work of God. A servant mind-set however is not natural and must be developed through the principles outlined in this opening section of chapter two.

Introduction

_____

_____

_____

I. Servants Must Mutilate _____ (vv. 2–3a)

PROVERBS 20:3

3   It is an honour for a man to cease from strife: but every fool will be meddling.

PROVERBS 17:19A

19   He loveth transgression that loveth strife…

A. We must be _____. (v. 2)

ROMANS 12:4–5

4   For as we have many members in one body, and all members have not the same office:

5   So we, being many, are one body in Christ, and every one members one of another.

EPHESIANS 4:3

3   Endeavouring to keep the unity of the Spirit in the bond of peace.

B. We must be _____. (v. 3a)

PROVERBS 13:10A

10   Only by pride cometh contention…

II. Servants Must Master _____ (vv. 3B–4)

A. *The enemy of* _____. *(v. 3B)*

JOHN 21:18–19A

18   *Verily, verily, I say unto thee, When thou wast young, thou girdest thyself, and walkedst whither thou wouldest: but when thou shalt be old, thou shalt stretch forth thy hands, and another shall gird thee, and carry thee whither thou wouldest not.*
19   *This spake he, signifying by what death he should glorify God.*

B. *The enemy of* _____. *(v. 4A)*

2 CORINTHIANS 10:17–18

17   *But he that glorieth, let him glory in the Lord.*
18   *For not he that commendeth himself is approved, but whom the Lord commendeth.*

C. *The enemy of* _____. *(v. 4B)*

1 KINGS 19:14

14   *And he said, I have been very jealous for the LORD God of hosts: because the children of Israel have forsaken thy covenant, thrown down thine altars, and slain thy prophets with the sword; and I, even I only, am left; and they seek my life, to take it away.*

III. Servants Must Have the Mind of the _____ (vv. 5–8)

PROVERBS 23:7A

7   *For as he thinketh in his heart, so is he…*

A. A _____ *mind (v. 5)*

2 PETER 1:4
4   *Whereby are given unto us exceeding great and precious promises: that by these ye might be partakers of the divine nature, having escaped the corruption that is in the world through lust.*

JEREMIAH 8:9
9   *The wise men are ashamed, they are dismayed and taken: lo, they have rejected the word of the Lord; and what wisdom is in them?*

B. A _____ *mind (vv. 6–7A)*

2 CHRONICLES 7:14A
14   *If my people, which are called by my name, shall **humble themselves**…* [Emphasis mine]

1 PETER 5:6
6   ***Humble yourselves** therefore under the mighty hand of God, that he may exalt you in due time:*

C. A _____ *mind (vv. 7B–8)*

Conclusion

_____

_____

_____

Study Questions

1. Where does strife originate? See Proverbs 13:10 and Romans 12:3.

2. Perhaps the second great sin after not giving glory to God is when in our pride we fail to acknowledge others who are faithfully serving God as well. Give one example from Scripture where someone in the Bible neglected to acknowledge another's service.

3. The Apostle Paul challenges us to give ourselves completely to God and tells us how to do so. According to Romans 12:1–2, how can we be transformed?

4. Are you a Philippians 1:21 Christian? Or, are you a Philippians 2:21 Christian? Read these verses, and explain your answer.

5. Carnal people make small problems bigger while spiritual people make big problems smaller. Pick out some problems you may have in your life. Think of your reaction to these problems. Are you making them bigger or smaller? Explain your answer.

6. Instead of complimenting others we often succumb to comparing ourselves with others. Ask God to bring three people to your mind who are in need of encouragement. List their names and how you can best compliment them. Memorize 2 Corinthians 10:12, and quote this verse every time you feel your mind starting to compare yourself with another.

7. As a Christian, you may want the right things—souls saved; revival in our churches; a solid, Christian home, etc.—but do you seek credit in the process? Read 1 Corinthians 4:6–7 and write a brief summary of Paul's thoughts in this passage of Scripture.

8. Self-centered pride characterizes the old nature (the person you were before salvation). But, the new nature is exemplified in a selfless service to Christ. If you want a miserable life, live for yourself, but if you want joy, what should you do?

Memory Verse

PHILIPPIANS 2:2

2 *Fulfil ye my joy, that ye be likeminded, having the same love, being of one accord, of one mind.*

A Name Exalted

Text

PHILIPPIANS 2:8–11

8 *And being found in fashion as a man, he humbled himself, and became obedient unto death, even the death of the cross.*

9 *Wherefore God also hath highly exalted him, and given him a name which is above every name:*

10 *That at the name of Jesus every knee should bow, of things in heaven, and things in earth, and things under the earth;*

11 *And that every tongue should confess that Jesus Christ is Lord, to the glory of God the Father.*

Overview

The name of Jesus Christ is the most honored and most hated name in the world. People don't mind if you mention God because they can interpret God to be whoever they want Him to be. But if Jesus Christ is Who He claims to be, then we are responsible for our sin and accountable to accept or reject Him. Those who accept Him find Him to be more than they could have imagined—their Saviour; Guide; Provider; Protector; Lord; and Friend. Those who love their sin too much to let Him into their life end up rejecting and cursing the name that is above all names. *"And this is the condemnation, that light is come into the world, and men loved darkness rather than light, because their deeds were evil. For every one that doeth evil hateth the light, neither cometh to the light, lest his deeds should be reproved"* (John 3:19–20).

Lesson Theme

We will focus in our lesson on why the name Jesus deserves our attention, love, and adoration. To associate ourselves as lowly sinners with the Son of God is both a privilege and responsibility. We bear His name and must live accordingly. *"Let every one that nameth the name of Christ depart from iniquity"* (2 Timothy 2:19B). When we identify with Christ, we must incorporate a new conduct.

Introduction

_____

_____

_____

1 JOHN 4:9–10, 19

9 In this was manifested the love of God toward us, because that God sent his only begotten Son into the world, that we might live through him.

10 Herein is love, not that we loved God, but that he loved us, and sent his Son to be the propitiation for our sins.

19 We love him, because he first loved us.

2 CORINTHIANS 5:15

15 And that he died for all, that they which live should not henceforth live unto themselves, but unto him which died for them, and rose again.

I.   The _____ for Exaltation (v. 8)

ACTS 4:12

12 Neither is their salvation in any other: for there is none other name under heaven given among men, whereby we must be saved.

JOHN 14:6B

6 ...I am the way, the truth, and the life: no man cometh unto the Father, but by me.

ISAIAH 43:11

11 I, even I, am the LORD; and beside me there is no saviour.

A. *A lowly* _____ (**v. 8A**)

B. *A loyal* _____ (**v. 8B**)

ROMANS 5:8

8   But God commendeth his love toward us, in that, *while we were yet sinners, Christ died for us.*

C. *A loving* _____ (**v. 8C**)

ISAIAH 50:6

6   *I gave my back to the smiters, and my cheeks to them that plucked off the hair: I hid not my face from shame and spitting.*

II. The _____ of Exaltation (vv. 9–10)

MATTHEW 3:16–17

16   *And Jesus, when he was baptized, went up straightway out of the water: and, lo, the heavens were opened unto him, and he saw the Spirit of God descending like a dove, and lighting upon him:*

17   *And lo a voice from heaven, saying, This is my beloved Son, in whom I am well pleased.*

A. *An honorary* _____ (**v. 9**)

ISAIAH 9:6

6   *For unto us a child is born, unto us a son is given: and the government shall be upon his shoulder: and his name shall be called Wonderful, Counsellor, The mighty God, The everlasting Father, The Prince of Peace.*

ISAIAH 42:8

8   I am the LORD: that is my name: and my glory will I not give to another, neither my praise to graven images.

PSALM 113:1–3

1   Praise ye the LORD. Praise, O ye servants of the LORD, praise the name of the LORD.

2   Blessed be the name of the LORD from this time forth and for evermore.

3   From the rising of the sun unto the going down of the same the LORD's name is to be praised.

B. A humble _____ (v. 10)

ECCLESIASTES 11:9

9   Rejoice, O young man, in thy youth; and let thy heart cheer thee in the days of thy youth, and walk in the ways of thine heart, and in the sight of thine eyes: but know thou, that for all these things God will bring thee into judgment.

III. The _____ of Exaltation (v. 11)

A. A universal _____ (v. 11A)

JOHN 5:22

22 For the Father judgeth no man, but hath committed all judgment unto the Son:

ACTS 17:31

31 Because he hath appointed a day, in the which he will judge the world in righteousness by that man whom he hath ordained; whereof he hath given

assurance unto all men, in that he hath raised him from the dead.

MALACHI 3:2A
2   But who may abide the day of his coming? and who shall stand when he appeareth? for he is like a refiner's fire...

B. A unanimous _____ *(v. 11B)*

ACTS 2:36
36   Therefore let all the house of Israel know assuredly, that God hath made that same Jesus, whom ye have crucified, both Lord and Christ.

C. An untarnished _____ *(v. 11C)*

1 PETER 4:11B
11   ...that God in all things may be glorified through Jesus Christ, to whom be praise and dominion for ever and ever. Amen.

Conclusion

_____

_____

_____

ROMANS 2:4
4   Or despisest thou the riches of his goodness and forbearance and longsuffering; not knowing that the goodness of God leadeth thee to repentance?

Study Questions

1. Using 1 John 4:9–10, explain how God showed His love to you.

2. Obeying is one thing, but when the requirement of that obedience is death, that takes the obedience to a whole new level. Jesus Christ obeyed His Father and was obedient unto death. But, for what specific reason did He die? See Romans 6:23, Romans 5:8, and Galatians 3:13.

3. What do the following verses say about the name of Jesus Christ: Philippians 2:9, Isaiah 42:8, and Isaiah 9:6?

4. What appointment do we have with God that we cannot cancel, reschedule, or miss? See Hebrews 9:27.

5. Have you praised the name of Jesus today? Read Psalm 113:1–3 and spend the next couple of moments praising the name of Jesus Christ.

6. Jesus Christ was more loyal to His Father than to His own will. He said, "...*I do always those things that please him*" (John 8:29B). Are you more loyal to the will of your Father than you are to your own will? Make a small list of your schedule for the next forty-eight hours. Review your list and ask yourself if everything on that list will please Him.

7. Because God has shown His love to us through His Son's death, we are to share His love with others. Ask God to burden your soul for those who do not yet know Christ as their personal Saviour. Make a prayer list of names who are not sure of salvation, and plan a time when you can share with them the true love of God. List those you can meet with this week, and list the specific times you can meet with them.

8. Spend some quiet time with the Lord and write out your personal testimony—the way you found salvation through Jesus Christ.

Memory Verse

PHILIPPIANS 2:10

10 *That at the name of Jesus every knee should bow, of things in heaven, and things in earth, and things under the earth;*

A Needed Examination

Text

PHILIPPIANS 2:12–18

12   Wherefore, my beloved, as ye have always obeyed, not as in my presence only, but now much more in my absence, work out your own salvation with fear and trembling.

13   For it is God which worketh in you both to will and to do of his good pleasure.

14   Do all things without murmurings and disputings:

15   That ye may be blameless and harmless, the sons of God, without rebuke, in the midst of a crooked and perverse nation, among whom ye shine as lights in the world;

16   Holding forth the word of life; that I may rejoice in the day of Christ, that I have not run in vain, neither laboured in vain.

17   Yea, and if I be offered upon the sacrifice and service of your faith, I joy, and rejoice with you all.

18   For the same cause also do ye joy, and rejoice with me.

Overview

These next several verses do not break down into an outline style quite as specifically as what we have done with previous verses, but there are six major emphases in this passage. Each one of them points to a specific area of our life that needs an examination to make sure that we are on track with God's plan for our life. If we are not in sync with God, the joy of the Lord is impossible. As the song says, "When we walk with the Lord, in the light of His Word; What a glory He sheds on our way..."

Lesson Theme

A faith that cannot be tested cannot be trusted. Our faith needs a test every so often to make sure that it is legitimate and matching up to God's expectations. The goal of joy presented in this book will never be attained unless we make sure from time to time that we are still going in God's direction. This lesson will help us match up the ideal of God with the reality of life.

Introduction

_____

_____

_____

Isaiah 34:16a
16 *Seek ye out of the book of the Lord, and read: no one of these shall fail...*

I. A Perpetual _____ (v. 12)

Proverbs 15:3
3 *The eyes of the Lord are in every place, beholding the evil and the good.*

2 Chronicles 16:9a
9 *For the eyes of the Lord run to and fro throughout the whole earth, to shew himself strong in the behalf of them whose heart is perfect toward him.*

1 Corinthians 15:58
58 *Therefore, my beloved brethren, be ye stedfast, unmoveable, always abounding in the work of the Lord, forasmuch as ye know that your labour is not in vain in the Lord.*

II. A Planned _____ (v. 13)

Psalm 37:23
23 *The steps of a good man are ordered by the Lord: and he delighteth in his way.*

Psalm 73:24

24 Thou shalt guide me with thy counsel, and afterward receive me to glory.

Isaiah 30:21

21 And thine ears shall hear a word behind thee, saying, This is the way, walk ye in it, when ye turn to the right hand, and when ye turn to the left.

III. A Pointed _____ (v. 14)

IV. A Perverse _____ (v. 15)

2 Timothy 3:13–14

13 But evil men and seducers shall wax worse and worse, deceiving, and being deceived.

14 But continue thou in the things which thou hast learned and hast been assured of, knowing of whom thou hast learned them;

V. A Powerful _____ (v. 16)

Isaiah 55:10–11

10 For as the rain cometh down, and the snow from heaven, and returneth not thither, but watereth the earth, and maketh it bring forth and bud, that it may give seed to the sower, and bread to the eater:

11 So shall my word be that goeth forth out of my mouth: it shall not return unto me void, but it shall accomplish that which I please, and it shall prosper in the thing whereto I sent it.

VI. A Praised _____ (vv. 17–18)

PSALM 128:1–2

1   Blessed is every one that feareth the LORD; that walketh in his ways.

2   For thou shalt eat the labour of thine hands: happy shalt thou be, and it shall be well with thee.

Conclusion

_____

_____

_____

Study Questions

1. List three people in the Bible who tried to hide from God.

2. How would you feel if Christ were to return today? Are you walking consistent with the truth of God's constant presence and His imminent return? List five things that you would do if you knew Christ would come back in the next week.

3. God's way and the devil's way both provide pleasure, but what is the difference between God's pleasure and the devil's pleasure?

4. What sin put more people to death than any other sin recorded in the Old Testament?

5. How is your spirit towards God? Do you dwell on what you don't have more than on God's blessings? List ten things for which you can thank God today.

6.   Do you blend in with this world, or can others see in your life the difference Christ makes? How can you let your light shine before men today?

7.   What will make your "light" effective in this perverse world?

8.   Where is true joy found? Write out Psalm 128:1–2.

Memory Verse

PHILIPPIANS 2:15

15   *That ye may be blameless and harmless, the sons of God, without rebuke, in the midst of a crooked and perverse nation, among whom ye shine as lights in the world;*

Two Notable Examples

Text

PHILIPPIANS 2:19–30

19 But I trust in the Lord Jesus to send Timotheus shortly unto you, that I also may be of good comfort, when I know your state.

20 For I have no man likeminded, who will naturally care for your state.

21 For all seek their own, not the things which are Jesus Christ's.

22 But ye know the proof of him, that, as a son with the father, he hath served with me in the gospel.

23 Him therefore I hope to send presently, so soon as I shall see how it will go with me.

24 But I trust in the Lord that I also myself shall come shortly.

25 Yet I supposed it necessary to send to you Epaphroditus, my brother, and companion in labour, and fellowsoldier, but your messenger, and he that ministered to my wants.

26 For he longed after you all, and was full of heaviness, because that ye had heard that he had been sick.

27 For indeed he was sick nigh unto death: but God had mercy on him; and not on him only, but on me also, lest I should have sorrow upon sorrow.

28 I sent him therefore the more carefully, that, when ye see him again, ye may rejoice, and that I may be the less sorrowful.

29 Receive him therefore in the Lord with all gladness; and hold such in reputation:

30 Because for the work of Christ he was nigh unto death, not regarding his life, to supply your lack of service toward me.

Overview

Every preacher or teacher knows the power of a timely illustration—something that sheds light on the truth so that it is more clearly seen. As chapter two closes, the Apostle Paul chooses to back up what he has been teaching with two examples that will serve as models to these believers. Someone has said, "A good example is worth a thousand sermons."

Lesson Theme

Because of their position in Christ, Paul is attempting to light a fire in these Christians that will never go out. He chooses to use two men as examples of faithfulness to show them that what he had taught them could be done. He points to their passion as well as their problems and how they endured through the good and bad to accomplish the will of God. Perhaps to appeal to the entire church he uses both a younger and an older Christian to encourage them and challenge them.

Introduction

_____

_____

_____

I. _____—A Son in the Faith (v. 19)

1 THESSALONIANS 3:5

5   *For this cause, when I could no longer forbear, I sent to know your faith, lest by some means the tempter have tempted you, and our labour be in vain.*

A. A _____ replaced a cause. (v. 20)

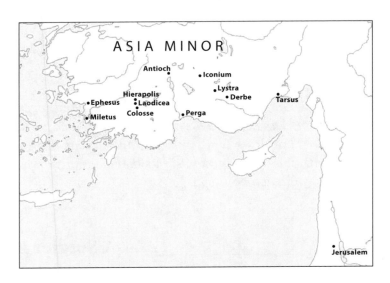

B. A _____ replaced a commitment. (v. 21)

GALATIANS 5:17

17 For the flesh lusteth against the Spirit, and the Spirit against the flesh: and these are contrary the one to the other: so that ye cannot do the things that ye would.

JUDE 24

24 Now unto him that is able to keep you from falling, and to present you faultless before the presence of his glory with exceeding joy,

C. A _____ replaced a compassion. (v. 22)

PROVERBS 14:23

23 In all labour there is profit: but the talk of the lips tendeth only to penury.

AMOS 6:1A, 4–6

1 Woe to them that are at ease in Zion…

4 That lie upon beds of ivory, and stretch themselves upon their couches, and eat the lambs out of the flock, and the calves out of the midst of the stall;

5 That chant to the sound of the viol, and invent to themselves instruments of musick, like David;

6 That drink wine in bowls, and anoint themselves with the chief ointments: but they are not grieved for the affliction of Joseph.

II. _____—A Soldier in the Fight (vv. 24–25A)

A. A walking _____ (v. 25A)

B. A wise _____ *(v. 25B)*

2 CORINTHIANS 5:17–20A

17 Therefore if any man be in Christ, he is a new creature: old things are passed away; behold, all things are become new.

18 And all things are of God, who hath reconciled us to himself by Jesus Christ, and hath given to us the ministry of reconciliation;

19 To wit, that God was in Christ, reconciling the world unto himself, not imputing their trespasses unto them; and hath committed unto us the word of reconciliation.

20 Now then we are ambassadors for Christ...

C. A willing _____ *(vv. 25C, 27)*

1 CORINTHIANS 16:15

15 I beseech you, brethren, (ye know the house of Stephanas, that it is the firstfruits of Achaia, and that they have addicted themselves to the ministry of the saints,)

D. A weary _____ *(vv. 28–30)*

Conclusion

_____

_____

_____

Study Questions

1. What two people does Paul use as an example for the believers at Philippi and how does he refer to each one?

2. The children of Israel were careless to let the culture's apathy seep into their church and their lives. Are you more consumed with life's comforts than the things of the Lord? What areas in your life do you see taking preeminence over God and His Word?

3. What does Jeremiah 17:9 say about your heart?

4. Ecclesiastes 5:4–6 tells the seriousness of every vow we make to God. List five commitments you have made to God in the past that you need to rededicate and commit to the Lord once again.

5. In what areas did you mimic Christ last week? List three areas in your life where you could be more conformed to His image this week.

6. God commands us to carry His Gospel of salvation to those who are lost. What are two things the Lord has used in your heart to compel you to be a witness for Him?

7. What does 1 Corinthians 16:15 say about the house of Stephanas?

8. Are you living your life as a godly example for others to see? What is one thing that God wants to change so you can be a better ambassador for Him?

Memory Verse

PHILIPPIANS 2:22

22 *But ye know the proof of him, that, as a son with the father, he hath served with me in the gospel.*

The Opposition of Our Joy

Text

PHILIPPIANS 3:1–2, 18–19

1 Finally, my brethren, rejoice in the Lord. To write the same things to you, to me indeed is not grievous, but for you it is safe.

2 Beware of dogs, beware of evil workers, beware of the concision.

18 (For many walk, of whom I have told you often, and now tell you even weeping, that they are the enemies of the cross of Christ:

19 Whose end is destruction, whose God is their belly, and whose glory is in their shame, who mind earthly things.)

Overview

Nothing moves without friction. If we are going to proceed on this journey of joy, there will always be something in our path to jeopardize our destination. Within chapter three of Philippians, Paul reminds us of our enemy, "lest Satan should get an advantage of us."

Lesson Theme

In athletics, the better prepared you are the better you'll play. Scouting reports are vital to good preparation. In this lesson, Paul gives us a scouting report on our enemy and how he will attempt to circumvent our joy. God's joy, unlike the world's, is not temporary. The devil, however, tries to block any momentum in our lives, by stealing our joy. Knowing what's coming can help us "snatch victory from the jaws of defeat."

Introduction

_____

_____

_____

I. Some Delayed _____ (v. 1)

A. Joy _____ through one _____. (v. 1A)

HEBREWS 13:5

5   Let your conversation be without covetousness; and be content with such things as ye have: for he hath said, I will never leave thee, nor forsake thee.

ROMANS 14:17

17   For the kingdom of God is not meat and drink; but righteousness, and peace, and joy in the Holy Ghost.

PSALM 16:11

11   Thou wilt shew me the path of life: in thy presence is fulness of joy; at thy right hand there are pleasures for evermore.

B. Joy _____ through ongoing _____. (v. 1B)

ISAIAH 28:9–10

9   Whom shall he teach knowledge? and whom shall he make to understand doctrine? them that are weaned from the milk, and drawn from the breasts.

10 For precept must be upon precept, precept upon precept; line upon line, line upon line; here a little, and there a little:

II. Some Deceptive _____ (v. 2)

2 CORINTHIANS 11:13–14
13 For such are false apostles, deceitful workers, transforming themselves into the apostles of Christ.
14 And no marvel; for Satan himself is transformed into an angel of light.

REVELATION 20:10A
10 And the devil that deceived them was cast into the lake of fire and brimstone…

A. Beware of _____. (v. 2A)

MATTHEW 26:33, 35
33 Peter answered and said unto him, Though all men shall be offended because of thee, yet will I never be offended.
35 Peter said unto him, Though I should die with thee, yet will I not deny thee. Likewise also said all the disciples.

1 CORINTHIANS 10:12
12 Wherefore let him that thinketh he standeth take heed lest he fall.

B. Beware of _____. (v. 2B)

C. Beware of _____. (v. 2C)

III. Some Destructive _____ (vv. 18–19)

A. Watch out for fleshly _____. (vv. 18–19A)

GALATIANS 5:24–26
24 And they that are Christ's have crucified the flesh with the affections and lusts.
25 If we live in the Spirit, let us also walk in the Spirit.
26 Let us not be desirous of vain glory, provoking one another, envying one another.

1 JOHN 2:16–17
16 For all that is in the world, the lust of the flesh, and the lust of the eyes, and the pride of life, is not of the Father, but is of the world.
17 And the world passeth away, and the lust thereof: but he that doeth the will of God abideth for ever.

B. Watch out for foolish _____. (v. 19B)

PROVERBS 25:27
27 It is not good to eat much honey: so for men to search their own glory is not glory.

C. Watch out for foreign _____. (v. 19C)

1 CORINTHIANS 6:12
12 All things are lawful unto me, but all things are not expedient: all things are lawful for me, but I will not be brought under the power of any.

JAMES 4:4

4   *Ye adulterers and adulteresses, know ye not that the friendship of the world is enmity with God? whosoever therefore will be a friend of the world is the enemy of God.*

Conclusion

_____

_____

_____

1 CORINTHIANS 10:13

13   *There hath no temptation taken you but such as is common to man: but God is faithful, who will not suffer you to be tempted above that ye are able; but will with the temptation also make a way to escape, that ye may be able to bear it.*

Study Questions

1. A joyful contentment is not found in our circumstances, but rather a Resource. Examine Hebrews 13:5, and describe the Resource found in this verse.

2. What is, perhaps, the devil's most effective and favorite weapon? See 2 Corinthians 11:13–14 and Revelation 20:10A.

3. The disciples forsook the Lord at His greatest time of need because they were inattentive when He pleaded with them to watch and pray. Describe some ways the Lord has gotten your attention in the past.

4. Paul tells us to beware of what three things mentioned in Philippians 3:2?

5. What one warning is proclaimed in each of these New Testament verses: 1 Corinthians 6:9, 1 Corinthians 15:33, and Galatians 6:7?

6. Look in the spiritual mirror. Are you still a baby Christian even though you may have been saved for awhile? Read 1 Corinthians 3:1–3 and then place yourself into the category of a "milk" Christian or a "meat" Christian. Explain why you would fit under that category.

7. A man knows more bad about himself than anyone else and yet he continues to think more highly of himself. Read the following verses, and write a small paragraph describing what the Bible has to say about a man's view of himself: Proverbs 25:27, Proverbs 17:19, Matthew 23:12, and Obadiah 4.

8. Read through a book in the Bible every day for twenty-five days. Choose a book like 1 John, and read it completely through every day for a month. If you determine to read through it with an open heart and a desire for God to teach you, you will learn something new every day. Write the book you have chosen to read.

Memory Verse

PHILIPPIANS 3:1

1 *Finally, my brethren, rejoice in the Lord. To write the same things to you, to me indeed is not grievous, but for you it is safe.*

The Obtaining of Our Justification

Text

PHILIPPIANS 3:3–9

3 For we are the circumcision, which worship God in the spirit, and rejoice in Christ Jesus, and have no confidence in the flesh.

4 Though I might also have confidence in the flesh. If any other man thinketh that he hath whereof he might trust in the flesh, I more:

5 Circumcised the eighth day, of the stock of Israel, of the tribe of Benjamin, an Hebrew of the Hebrews; as touching the law, a Pharisee;

6 Concerning zeal, persecuting the church; touching the righteousness which is in the law, blameless.

7 But what things were gain to me, those I counted loss for Christ.

8 Yea doubtless, and I count all things but loss for the excellency of the knowledge of Christ Jesus my Lord: for whom I have suffered the loss of all things, and do count them but dung, that I may win Christ,

9 And be found in him, not having mine own righteousness, which is of the law, but that which is through the faith of Christ, the righteousness which is of God by faith:

Overview

This section of verses contains the testimony of the Apostle Paul and shares the Gospel. Paul was a very religious man, but lost until he had an unusual encounter with the Lord on the road to Damascus. Paul was as zealous in his attempt to stamp out Christianity before he got saved as he was to propagate the Gospel after he met the Lord. People today put their hearts in all kinds of things, but God wants to change their lives and use them for His glory.

Lesson Theme

This lesson provides a great opportunity to accomplish two purposes. First to explain salvation—what it is and what it isn't. Second, to help us in our witness to others. It also teaches that we must never give up on people even if they are steeped in religion or their own stubborn ways of thinking. Paul was such a man that God was able to change.

Introduction

_____

_____

_____

LUKE 10:20
20 *Notwithstanding in this rejoice not, that the spirits are subject unto you; but rather rejoice, because your names are written in heaven.*

I. A Following of _____ (vv. 3–6)

A. *An impressive _____ (vv. 3–4)*

ISAIAH 64:6–7A
6 *But we are all as an unclean thing, and all our righteousnesses are as filthy rags; and we all do fade as a leaf; and our iniquities, like the wind, have taken us away.*
7 *And there is none that calleth upon thy name, that stirreth up himself to take hold of thee:...*

EPHESIANS 2:2–3
2 *Wherein in time past ye walked according to the course of this world, according to the prince of the power of the air, the spirit that now worketh in the children of disobedience:*
3 *Among whom also we all had our conversation in times past in the lusts of our flesh, fulfilling the desires of the flesh and of the mind; and were **by nature** the children of wrath, even as others.* [Emphasis mine]

B. An institutional _____ *(v. 5)*

C. An incredible _____ *(v. 6B)*

II. A Facilitation of _____ (vv. 5–6)

A. A cherished _____ *(v. 5A)*

B. A chosen _____ *(v. 5B)*

EZEKIEL 18:20

20 *The soul that sinneth, it shall die. The son shall not bear the iniquity of the father, neither shall the father bear the iniquity of the son: the righteousness of the righteous shall be upon him, and the wickedness of the wicked shall be upon him.*

PROVERBS 27:1

1 *Boast not thyself of to morrow; for thou knowest not what a day may bring forth.*

C. A chilling _____ *(v. 6A)*

ACTS 9:1–5

1 *And Saul, yet breathing out threatenings and slaughter against the disciples of the Lord, went unto the high priest,*

2 *And desired of him letters to Damascus to the synagogues, that if he found any of this way, whether they were men or women, he might bring them bound unto Jerusalem.*

3   And as he journeyed, he came near Damascus: and suddenly there shined round about him a light from heaven:

4   And he fell to the earth, and heard a voice saying unto him, Saul, Saul, why persecutest thou me?

5   And he said, Who art thou, Lord? And the Lord said, I am Jesus whom thou persecutest: it is hard for thee to kick against the pricks.

2 CORINTHIANS 5:17

17   Therefore if any man be in Christ, he is a new creature: old things are passed away; behold, all things are become new.

III. A Faith in _____ (vv. 7–9)

A. *The acknowledgement of a* _____ *(v. 7)*

B. *The abandonment of a* _____ *(v. 8)*

LUKE 13:3

3   I tell you, Nay: but, except ye repent, ye shall all likewise perish.

2 PETER 3:9

*9   The Lord is not slack concerning his promise, as some men count slackness; but is longsuffering to us-ward, not willing that any should perish, **but that all should come to repentance.***

C. *The acceptance of a* _____ *(v. 9)*

GALATIANS 2:21

21 I do not frustrate the grace of God: for if righteousness come by the law, then Christ is dead in vain.

Conclusion

_____

_____

_____

1 JOHN 5:11–13

11 And this is the record, that God hath given to us eternal life, and this life is in his Son.

12 He that hath the Son hath life; and he that hath not the Son of God hath not life.

13 These things have I written unto you that believe on the name of the Son of God; that ye may know that ye have eternal life, and that ye may believe on the name of the Son of God.

Study Questions

1. What does the Bible compare our righteousness to in Isaiah 64:6–7A?

2. According to Psalm 51:5, what was David born with?

3. Describe the outside appearance of a Pharisee. Refer to Luke 18:10–11.

4. Using Titus 3:5–6, how would you respond to this statement: I believe that because I am a good person, God will let me into Heaven?

5. Paul listed reasons why he was confident in his flesh before his conversion. What were these reasons? Refer to Philippians 3:5–6.

6. When God saves us, it is not an overhaul of the old, but a complete doing away with the old and giving us a brand new heart, a brand new spirit, a brand new life! At the moment of salvation, this radical change takes place through faith. Write out Romans 3:24–28—the process of salvation through faith.

7. Choice, not chance, determines a man's destiny. Salvation is a choice given by God and left in your hands. According to the Scriptures, when does God want you to make your choice regarding salvation? See 2 Corinthians 6:2B, Psalm 95:7B–8A, and Proverbs 27:1.

8. Perhaps the hardest thing a person does at salvation is abandon what he has previously trusted in to save him. What do you put your trust in for salvation from sin and sin's payment? Read John 11:25–26 and answer the question at the end of verse 26.

Memory Verse

PHILIPPIANS 3:8

8 *Yea doubtless, and I count all things but loss for the excellency of the knowledge of Christ Jesus my Lord: for whom I have suffered the loss of all things, and do count them but dung, that I may win Christ,*

The Objective of Our Journey

Text

PHILIPPIANS 3:10–14, 20–21

10 *That I may know him, and the power of his resurrection, and the fellowship of his sufferings, being made conformable unto his death;*

11 *If by any means I might attain unto the resurrection of the dead.*

12 *Not as though I had already attained, either were already perfect: but I follow after, if that I may apprehend that for which also I am apprehended of Christ Jesus.*

13 *Brethren, I count not myself to have apprehended: but this one thing I do, forgetting those things which are behind, and reaching forth unto those things which are before,*

14 *I press toward the mark for the prize of the high calling of God in Christ Jesus.*

20 *For our conversation is in heaven; from whence also we look for the Saviour, the Lord Jesus Christ:*

21 *Who shall change our vile body, that it may be fashioned like unto his glorious body, according to the working whereby he is able even to subdue all things unto himself.*

Overview

The Christian life is one of growth and progress toward the goal of becoming like Christ. The longer we are saved, the more we should resemble our heavenly Father. When we first get saved, our lives will still have a lot of the baggage of the world, but each day some of that baggage should fall by the wayside and our walk with Christ should grow stronger. *"And when he had called the people unto him with his disciples also, he said unto them, Whosoever will come after me, let him deny himself, and take up his cross, and follow me"* (Mark 8:34).

Lesson Theme

Salvation is called the "new birth" and is the starting point for our walk with Christ. Sanctification is the process of growth as our lives are changed into the image of Christ. While sin and the flesh once dominated and directed our lives prior to salvation, now the Word of God and the Holy Spirit are in place to direct us to become like Him. This process of growth doesn't take place automatically however. We must choose to eat and exercise our spiritual life in order to become all that He intends for our lives.

Introduction

_____

_____

_____

I. _____ about Christ (v. 10)

A. *Learning about His* _____ *(v. 10A)*

ROMANS 1:4

4   And declared to be the Son of God with power, according to the spirit of holiness, by the resurrection from the dead:

PSALM 62:11

11   God hath spoken once; twice have I heard this; that power belongeth unto God.

B. *Learning about His* _____ *(v. 10B)*

C. *Learning about His* _____ *(v. 10C)*

REVELATION 4:11

11   Thou art worthy, O Lord, to receive glory and honour and power: for thou hast created all things, and for thy pleasure they are and were created.

ISAIAH 26:3–4

3   Thou wilt keep him in perfect peace, whose mind is stayed on thee: because he trusteth in thee.

4   Trust ye in the LORD for ever: for in the LORD JEHOVAH is everlasting strength:

II. _____ toward Christ (vv. 12–14)

A. _____ *the past (vv. 12–13)*

Luke 9:62

62 And Jesus said unto him, No man, having put his hand to the plough, and looking back, is fit for the kingdom of God.

Proverbs 16:18

18 Pride goeth before destruction, and an haughty spirit before a fall.

B. _____ *for the prize (v. 14A)*

1 Corinthians 9:24–25

24 Know ye not that they which run in a race run all, but one receiveth the prize? So run, that ye may obtain.

25 And every man that striveth for the mastery is temperate in all things. Now they do it to obtain a corruptible crown; but we an incorruptible.

2 Timothy 4:7–8

7 I have fought a good fight, I have finished my course, I have kept the faith:

8 Henceforth there is laid up for me a crown of righteousness, which the Lord, the righteous judge, shall give me at that day: and not to me only, but unto all them also that love his appearing.

2 John 8

8 Look to yourselves, that we lose not those things which we have wrought, but that we receive a full reward.

C. _____ *on the person (v. 14B)*

EPHESIANS 6:6–7

6   *Not with eyeservice, as menpleasers; but as the servants of Christ, doing the will of God from the heart;*

7   *With good will doing service, as to the Lord, and not to men:*

III. _____ for Christ (vv. 20–21)

JOHN 14:1–3

1   *Let not your heart be troubled: ye believe in God, believe also in me.*

2   *In my Father's house are many mansions: if it were not so, I would have told you. I go to prepare a place for you.*

3   *And if I go and prepare a place for you, I will come again, and receive you unto myself; that where I am, there ye may be also.*

A. *Our _____ is temporary. (v. 20A)*

1 THESSALONIANS 4:13–18

13   *But I would not have you to be ignorant, brethren, concerning them which are asleep, that ye sorrow not, even as others which have no hope.*

14   *For if we believe that Jesus died and rose again, even so them also which sleep in Jesus will God bring with him.*

15   *For this we say unto you by the word of the Lord, that we which are alive and remain unto the coming of the Lord shall not prevent them which are asleep.*

16 For the Lord himself shall descend from heaven with a shout, with the voice of the archangel, and with the trump of God: and the dead in Christ shall rise first:

17 Then we which are alive and remain shall be caught up together with them in the clouds, to meet the Lord in the air: and so shall we ever be with the Lord.

18 Wherefore comfort one another with these words.

B. Our _____ is temporary. (v. 20B)

1 CORINTHIANS 13:12

12 For now we see through a glass, darkly; but then face to face: now I know in part; but then shall I know even as also I am known.

C. Our _____ is temporary. (v. 21)

Conclusion

_____

_____

_____

Study Questions

1. According to Philippians 3:10, what is one of the first steps and objectives in having a life of joy?

2. As we study Philippians 3:10, we learn of the power of Christ. Jesus has the power to not only save us, but to also deliver us from everyday habits and trials. In what area of your life do you need the power of Christ? Take a moment to pray and claim His power in that particular area.

3. Look up and write out the definition for the following words: preeminent and prominent. Describe how Christ should have the preeminence in our lives.

4. According to our text, leaning on Christ involves forgetting the past. What two aspects of our past should we choose to forget?

5. What did Epaphras pray for the church at Colosse as recorded in Colossians 4:12? How does this verse relate to fighting for the prize of the high calling of God?

6. In Daniel 5:18–21 and Acts 1:21–23, we find two biblical examples of men who focused on the wrong person. Who were they?

7. As we look for Christ in our daily lives, we understand that this world is temporary. What three specific aspects of our lives are temporary?

8. The objective of our journey is to become more like Christ. What three actions will help us conform to His image?

Memory Verse

PHILIPPIANS 3:13

13 Brethren, I count not myself to have apprehended: but this one thing I do, forgetting those things which are behind, and reaching forth unto those things which are before,

Loving Your Co-Laborers

Text

PHILIPPIANS 4:1–5

1   *Therefore, my brethren dearly beloved and longed for, my joy and crown, so stand fast in the Lord, my dearly beloved.*

2   *I beseech Euodias, and beseech Syntyche, that they be of the same mind in the Lord.*

3   *And I intreat thee also, true yokefellow, help those women which laboured with me in the gospel, with Clement also, and with other my fellowlabourers, whose names are in the book of life.*

4   *Rejoice in the Lord alway: and again I say, Rejoice.*

5   *Let your moderation be known unto all men. The Lord is at hand.*

Overview

One of the missing yet vital aspects among God's people today is unity. *"Behold, how good and how pleasant it is for brethren to dwell together in unity!"* (Psalm 133:1). God has made each of us different in talent and personality, but He commands us to labor together in the harvest. Too often the harvest is lost because the laborers are fighting among themselves about who does which jobs and who will receive the credit.

Lesson Theme

Sadly those with whom we ought to have great commonality, often become a source of contention and strife. Being at odds with a brother or sister in Christ is never spiritual, but rather "earthly, sensual, and devilish." The local church is God's vehicle to accomplish His work on earth today. When there is strife within that body of believers, the wheels will soon come off and the vehicle that is empowered by the Spirit of the living God is left immobilized on the side of the road. Paul in this lesson warns the believer of the potential disaster that awaits the church in disharmony.

Introduction

_____

_____

_____

I. Beware of an _____ Spirit (v. 1)

1 John 3:14a
14 We know that we have passed from death unto life, because we love the brethren.

1 John 3:18
18 My little children, let us not love in word, neither in tongue; but in deed and in truth.

Proverbs 16:7
7 When a man's ways please the Lord, he maketh even his enemies to be at peace with him.

II. Beware of an _____ Spirit (v. 2)

Ephesians 4:30–32
30 And grieve not the holy Spirit of God, whereby ye are sealed unto the day of redemption.
31 Let all bitterness, and wrath, and anger, and clamour, and evil speaking, be put away from you, with all malice:
32 And be ye kind one to another, tenderhearted, forgiving one another, even as God for Christ's sake hath forgiven you.

PROVERBS 26:21

21 *As coals are to burning coals, and wood to fire; so is a contentious man to kindle strife.*

JAMES 3:14–16

14 *But if ye have bitter envying and strife in your hearts, glory not, and lie not against the truth.*

15 *This wisdom descendeth not from above, but is earthly, sensual, and devilish.*

16 *For where envying and strife is, there is confusion and every evil work.*

III. Beware of an _____ Spirit (v. 3)

ROMANS 1:21A

21 *Because that, when they knew God, they glorified him not as God, neither were thankful...*

IV. Beware of an _____ Spirit (v. 4)

DEUTERONOMY 33:29A

29 *Happy art thou, O Israel: who is like unto thee, O people saved by the LORD...*

PSALM 144:15

15 *Happy is that people, that is in such a case: yea, happy is that people, whose God is the LORD.*

PSALM 146:5

5 *Happy is he that hath the God of Jacob for his help, whose hope is in the LORD his God:*

V. Beware of an _____ Spirit (v. 5A)

VI. Beware of an _____ Spirit (v. 5B)

MARK 13:32–33; 35–37

32 But of that day and that hour knoweth no man, no, not the angels which are in heaven, neither the Son, but the Father.

33 Take ye heed, watch and pray: for ye know not when the time is.

35 Watch ye therefore: for ye know not when the master of the house cometh, at even, or at midnight, or at the cockcrowing, or in the morning:

36 Lest coming suddenly he find you sleeping.

37 And what I say unto you I say unto you all, Watch.

Conclusion

_____

_____

_____

Study Questions

1. The Greek language has three words for love: eros, phileo, and agape. Christ loves us with what kind of love and what is the definition of that love?

2. According to John 13:34–35, what is the greatest testimony we have for Christ in this world?

3. In Philippians 4:2, we find two men who were rebuked for their upset spirit. What were their names?

4. Paul admonishes the Philippians to help and remember those who have labored in the Gospel (Philippians 4:3). We must also beware of an unappreciative spirit. Take a moment to list five things for which you may have forgotten to be thankful.

5. The theme for the book of Philippians is stated in chapter four, verse four. Write out the verse in the space provided below.

6. Describe the Apostle Paul's spirit as recorded in 2 Corinthians 12:8–10.

7. According to Philippians 4:5A, to whom should our moderation (forbearance/forgiveness) be known? Is there a person who has not experienced your forgiveness, but who needs to? If so, take a moment right now to make that right.

8. What is the greatest motivator in loving our co-laborers (Philippians 4:5B)?

Memory Verse

PHILIPPIANS 4:4
4   *Rejoice in the Lord alway: and again I say, Rejoice.*

Living with Your Circumstances

Text

PHILIPPIANS 4:6–9

6   Be careful for nothing; but in every thing by prayer and supplication with thanksgiving let your requests be made known unto God.

7   And the peace of God, which passeth all understanding, shall keep your hearts and minds through Christ Jesus.

8   Finally, brethren, whatsoever things are true, whatsoever things are honest, whatsoever things are just, whatsoever things are pure, whatsoever things are lovely, whatsoever things are of good report; if there be any virtue, and if there be any praise, think on these things.

9   Those things, which ye have both learned, and received, and heard, and seen in me, do: and the God of peace shall be with you.

Overview

People often blame the problems in their life on their circumstances or the environment in which they live. Contemporary counseling often encourages people to assume that nothing can change in our lives until our circumstances change. This is completely contradictory to what the Bible teaches. Job certainly found himself in some adverse circumstances that were no fault of his own. But when his wife chided him to "Curse God and die," his response was, "…Thou speakest as one of the foolish women speaketh. What? shall we receive good at the hand of God, and *shall we not receive evil? In all this did not Job sin with his lips"* (Job 2:10).

Lesson Theme

Bad choices will leave us with some bad circumstances. On the other hand, there are times when God chooses for us to go through a fiery trial. How we respond in those circumstances indicates what is in us. Without God's grace we will never survive the tests of life. With His grace we can find blessing and victories in the most adverse conditions. This lesson will help us develop a strategy for those rough times of life.

Introduction

_____

_____

_____

I. _____ Is the Answer (v. 6)

A. *Prayer _____ all (v. 6A)*

1 JOHN 5:14–15
14 And this is the confidence that we have in him, that, if we ask any thing according to his will, he heareth us:

15 And if we know that he hear us, whatsoever we ask, we know that we have the petitions that we desired of him.

B. *Prayer _____ appreciation (v. 6B)*

COLOSSIANS 4:2
2 Continue in prayer, and watch in the same with thanksgiving;

EPHESIANS 5:20
20 Giving thanks always for all things unto God and the Father in the name of our Lord Jesus Christ;

C. *Prayer _____ asking (v. 6C)*

MATTHEW 7:7
7 Ask, and it shall be given you…

JAMES 4:2
2 …ye have not, because ye ask not.

II. _____ Is the Anticipation (v. 7)

ISAIAH 57:20–21

20 But the wicked are like the troubled sea, when it cannot rest, whose waters cast up mire and dirt.

21 There is no peace, saith my God, to the wicked.

EZEKIEL 7:25

25 Destruction cometh; and they shall seek peace, and there shall be none.

JOHN 16:33

33 These things I have spoken unto you, that in me ye might have peace. In the world ye shall have tribulation: but be of good cheer; I have overcome the world.

A. The _____ of peace (v. 7A)

JOHN 14:27

27 Peace I leave with you, my peace I give unto you: not as the world giveth, give I unto you. Let not your heart be troubled, neither let it be afraid.

PSALM 29:11

11 The LORD will give strength unto his people; the LORD will bless his people with peace.

ROMANS 5:1

1 Therefore being justified by faith, we have peace with God through our Lord Jesus Christ:

ISAIAH 48:18

18 O that thou hadst hearkened to my commandments! then had thy peace been as a river, and thy righteousness as the waves of the sea:

B. The _____ **of peace (v. 7b)**

C. The _____ **of peace (v. 7c)**

NUMBERS 23:19

19   God is not a man, that he should lie; neither the son of man, that he should repent: hath he said, and shall he not do it? or hath he spoken, and shall he not make it good?

PROVERBS 3:24

24   When thou liest down, thou shalt not be afraid: yea, thou shalt lie down, and thy sleep shall be sweet.

PSALM 91:5

5   Thou shalt not be afraid for the terror by night; nor for the arrow that flieth by day;

ISAIAH 46:4

4   And even to your old age I am he; and even to hoar hairs will I carry you: I have made, and I will bear; even I will carry, and will deliver you.

III. _____ Is the Antecedent (vv. 8–9)

A. The discipline of _____ **thoughts (v. 8)**

PROVERBS 23:7A

7   For as he thinketh in his heart, so is he…

PROVERBS 4:23

23   Keep thy heart with all diligence; for out of it are the issues of life.

GALATIANS 5:17

17 For the flesh lusteth against the Spirit, and the Spirit against the flesh: and these are contrary the one to the other: so that ye cannot do the things that ye would.

B. *The development of* _____ *tasks (v. 9)*

Conclusion

_____

_____

_____

Study Questions

1. What is the answer to living with our circumstances?

2. What is one key attribute that our prayer should contain (Philippians 4:6b)?

3. Prayer covers all and should contain appreciation, but simply stated, what is prayer (Matthew 7:7)?

4. Philippians 4:6 exhorts us to let our requests be made known unto God. Take a moment to list a few specific requests to the Lord, and then take time to ask God to meet those needs.

5. According to Philippians 4:7a, who is our Source of peace?

6. Look up Isaiah 26:3. What type of peace does God promise to those whose minds are fixed on Him?

7. Look up the word "antecedent" in a dictionary and write the definition below.

8. According to our lesson, what preceding actions must we take to experience God's peace in our lives?

Memory Verse

PHILIPPIANS 4:6

6 *Be careful for nothing; but in every thing by prayer and supplication with thanksgiving let your requests be made known unto God.*

Learning Contentment

Text

PHILIPPIANS 4:10–19

10 But I rejoiced in the Lord greatly, that now at the last your care of me hath flourished again; wherein ye were also careful, but ye lacked opportunity.

11 Not that I speak in respect of want: for I have learned, in whatsoever state I am, therewith to be content.

12 I know both how to be abased, and I know how to abound: every where and in all things I am instructed both to be full and to be hungry, both to abound and to suffer need.

13 I can do all things through Christ which strengtheneth me.

14 Notwithstanding ye have well done, that ye did communicate with my affliction.

15 Now ye Philippians know also, that in the beginning of the gospel, when I departed from Macedonia, no church communicated with me as concerning giving and receiving, but ye only.

16 For even in Thessalonica ye sent once and again unto my necessity.

17 Not because I desire a gift: but I desire fruit that may abound to your account.

18 But I have all, and abound: I am full, having received of Epaphroditus the things which were sent from you, an odour of a sweet smell, a sacrifice acceptable, wellpleasing to God.

19 But my God shall supply all your need according to his riches in glory by Christ Jesus.

Overview

Contentment is not natural nor is it encouraged in our busy twenty-first century world. Our selfish lifestyles yearn for constant change. We are not happy with ourselves much less the conditions around us. As a result, the child of God must grow away from a restless spirit to a resigned spirit, contented in God's will.

Lesson Theme.

Paul had to "learn" contentment. As human beings we blame our restless spirits on our circumstances, but Paul teaches us here that it is the circumstances that come our way that are designed by God to teach us to be content. This lesson is designed to direct our eyes off of the situations of life and to the One who is behind those situations and in control. We are never left alone or outside of God's protective care.

Introduction

_____

_____

_____

HEBREWS 13:5

5   *Let your conversation be without covetousness: and be content with such things as ye have: for he hath said, I will never leave thee, nor forsake thee.*

I.   The Undaunted _____ of God (v. 11)

A.   *Life's _____ do not dictate God's _____.*

B.   *Life's _____ do not dilute God's _____.*

ROMANS 8:35–39

35   Who shall separate us from the love of Christ? shall tribulation, or distress, or persecution, or famine, or nakedness, or peril, or sword?

36   As it is written, For thy sake we are killed all the day long; we are accounted as sheep for the slaughter.

37   Nay, in all these things we are more than conquerors through him that loved us.

38   For I am persuaded, that neither death, nor life, nor angels, nor principalities, nor powers, nor things present, nor things to come,

39 Nor height, nor depth, nor any other creature, shall be able to separate us from the love of God, which is in Christ Jesus our Lord.

C. Life's _____ do not delete God's _____.

1 SAMUEL 15:22–24

22 And Samuel said, Hath the LORD as great delight in burnt offerings and sacrifices, as in obeying the voice of the LORD? Behold, to obey is better than sacrifice, and to hearken than the fat of rams.

23 For rebellion is as the sin of witchcraft, and stubbornness is as iniquity and idolatry. Because thou hast rejected the word of the LORD, he hath also rejected thee from being king.

24 And Saul said unto Samuel, I have sinned: for I have transgressed the commandment of the LORD, and thy words: because I feared the people, and obeyed their voice.

II. The Unfailing _____ of God (v. 13)

ISAIAH 40:12–18

12 Who hath measured the waters in the hollow of his hand, and meted out heaven with the span, and comprehended the dust of the earth in a measure, and weighed the mountains in scales, and the hills in a balance?

13 Who hath directed the Spirit of the LORD, or being his counsellor hath taught him?

14 With whom took he counsel, and who instructed him, and taught him in the path of judgment, and taught him knowledge, and shewed to him the way of understanding?

15   Behold, the nations are as a drop of a bucket, and are counted as the small dust of the balance: behold, he taketh up the isles as a very little thing.

16   And Lebanon is not sufficient to burn, nor the beasts thereof sufficient for a burnt offering.

17   All nations before him are as nothing; and they are counted to him less than nothing, and vanity.

18   To whom then will ye liken God? or what likeness will ye compare unto him?

A. *This is an _____ power.*

GENESIS 21:1–2

1   And the LORD visited Sarah as he had said, and the LORD did unto Sarah as he had spoken.

2   For Sarah conceived, and bare Abraham a son in his old age, at the set time of which God had spoken to him.

B. *This is an _____ power.*

PSALM 8:3–4

3   When I consider thy heavens, the work of thy fingers, the moon and the stars, which thou hast ordained;

4   What is man, that thou art mindful of him? and the son of man, that thou visitest him?

ISAIAH 40:29

29   He giveth power to the faint; and to them that have no might he increaseth strength.

C. This is an _____ **power.**

JOHN 6:63

63 It is the spirit that quickeneth; the flesh profiteth nothing: the words that I speak unto you, they are spirit, and they are life.

ZECHARIAH 4:6

6 Then he answered and spake unto me, saying, This is the word of the LORD unto Zerubbabel, saying, Not by might, nor by power, but by my spirit, saith the LORD of hosts.

III. The Unchanging _____ of God (v. 19)

A. God's promises cover _____ _____. **(vv. 15–16)**

PSALM 37:25

25 I have been young, and now am old; yet have I not seen the righteous forsaken, nor his seed begging bread.

B. God's promises cover _____ _____. **(v. 18)**

PROVERBS 27:17

17 Iron sharpeneth iron; so a man sharpeneth the countenance of his friend.

PROVERBS 13:20

20 He that walketh with wise men shall be wise: but a companion of fools shall be destroyed.

PROVERBS 18:24A

24 A man that hath friends must shew himself friendly...

PROVERBS 25:21–22

21 If thine enemy be hungry, give him bread to eat; and if he be thirsty, give him water to drink:
22 For thou shalt heap coals of fire upon his head, and the LORD shall reward thee.

C. God's promises cover _____
_____. (v. 17)

ISAIAH 41:10

10 Fear thou not; for I am with thee: be not dismayed; for I am thy God: I will strengthen thee; yea, I will help thee; yea, I will uphold thee with the right hand of my righteousness.

1 THESSALONIANS 5:16

16 Rejoice evermore.

Conclusion

_____

_____

_____

Study Questions

1. What does God tell us to do with our burdens according to 1 Peter 5:7?

2. Read Romans 8:35–39. After reading these verses, describe God's love and compassion for you.

3. Often, we come to changes in our lives and think that the changes delete God's commands to us. Take a moment to list an area in which you need to heed God's commandments, no matter what life changes may come. (Read 1 Samuel 15 for further reference.)

4. Look up the definitions for the following words and notate how they relate to God's power: inclusive and invested.

5. Contentment comes when we rely on His power, rather than our own. Name an Old Testament example of one who allowed God's power to work in him.

6. As mentioned in the lesson, God's promises cover three major aspects of our lives. What are they?

7. God promises to supply not all of our greeds, but all of our needs. List two or three specific needs you are facing right now, and claim God's promise to meet those needs.

8. God's promises cover ministry desires. What desires do you have for your ministry, whether it be in the area of personal soulwinning or involvement in your local church? Take a moment to write out five personal ministry goals, and again, claim God's abundant promises to see fruit that will be added to your account.

Memory Verse

PHILIPPIANS 4:11

11 *Not that I speak in respect of want: for I have learned, in whatsoever state I am, therewith to be content.*

For additional Christian
growth resources visit
www.strivingtogether.com